What Only a Pen Could Say

A Collection of 32 Poems and Epics on Love, Loss, Controversy, and Becoming

By: KaLaura O'Ram

What Only a Pen Could Say

Dedication

To my son, Nezaryi,

May you find comfort in the lessons I've already learned so you don't feel alone in your journey. I pray courage and a strong sense of self over you. I will continue to raise you to see the world through the lens of creation and not destruction.

This journey I have been on has prepared me to uplift you into your destiny, to carry the torch for those who come after.

I will see you through to your last days, even when I no longer breathe.

You will change the world long after I am gone.

I walk within and beside you, always.

Remember: you are one man of many who came before you. A nation walks within you.

You are my life, my line, and everything in between.

I love you and every phase of you, my padawan.

To you, I dedicate my first published piece.

Table of Contents

Part II: Inheriting Fire

Part III: The Call Is from Inside

Part I:

Bleeding Passion

This section explores the bridges of intimacy. It's the perspectives of passion, all different but known to us in one form or another. The reminder that depth is apart of human nature. The territory of love, lust, anger, happiness, commitment, uncertainty, confidence and jealousy explored here through the lens of many.

1.

Unspoken

My words bleed beautifully on the page.
It is in these moments with myself
when unspoken words feel safe.

The freedom to start a new page,
one I can erase.
Here I am free to make mistakes.

To take a new turn.
I can rip up the page,
set it on fire,
and watch it burn.

In the company of my pen and page,
my words and I are never alone.

After all,
they were always mine to own.

2.

Growing Hands

Growing hands,

that's my man.

He grew our love from seed to bloom
with patient, intentional hands.

He changed me.
Empowered me.
I protect him.
He protects me.

We are synchronized in sacred union.
Halves of two, moving as one—
synergy.

Yet we hold our individuality.

He falls for every version of me.
He learned me.
Relearned me.
And still, he yearns for me.

We did not get here without scars.
But he does not take without giving.

I flinched at love,
afraid it would bruise—
but his hands.
Strong hands.
Gentle hands.

Held space for me
He defends my honor,
captures my soul,
and paints murals
on the beaten door of my heart.

Only those hands
could turn something so painful
into a beautiful work of art.

With those growing hands,
he repairs my heart.

Our love was destined to be magical
from the very start.
It was written in the stars.

From your love,
I will never part.

3.
Sincerely Yours

You are air, so free.
Even when I am alone,
I know you are all around me.

Take me to your inner plane.
I want to live in you.
To be loved by you.

A muse for your spirit,
and together we inspire.
Everything the light touches
becomes our empire.

Bring me your heart,
and we will beat as one.
Your wish is my command.
So, thy will be done.

A soldier of love,
for your love.
Fearlessly, we march to the beat of your drums.

Your essence — intoxicating.
No — invigorating.
The epitome of divine.
And what is time to a love so immortal?

Energy only transforms.
I feel you in every dimension.
I feel you all around me,
like the wind in the leaves
You breeze through me.
You carry me from earth
to our origin land in the stars.

I will bring you Venus,
tied to a golden chariot.
Bound by your gravity,
take from me all you can carry.

I was made to please you.
I was made to ease you.
I am yours.

4.

Her Pleasure

"You are a moment untouched by time."
I say to myself,
as I wrap your curls around my fingers
like thread pulled from a dream.

Marvin Gaye spills into candlelit silence
as I watch your body sway from behind,
to the rhythm of us.

I fit perfectly in you.

Like a brush to canvas,
I trace your spine with reverence,
admiring each stretch mark.
It feels as if Van Gogh painted you himself.

Is this real,
or just the dream your body keeps drawing me into?
The way you take my mind
feels more surreal the longer we go.

I turn you over.

Your soft melody of pleasure
says more than any words could.
No sweeter than the melody
that falls from my own lips.

I am not afraid to say your name.
You awaken me.

I make love to every part of you —
your mental,
your physical,
your spiritual

Your body calls to mine,
asking me to pull you closer,
to let you feel all of me,
to make you feel like I will never let you go.

I listen.

Your body tells me to go deeper.
And I do.

I rise in your iridescent oasis.
The more I listen,
the further we float.

I push deeper,
swimming inside the spring of your spirit.

I want to whisper in your ear
how whole I feel in this moment.

I lean into the nape of your neck
and let out one soft, powerful breath.
I feel your baby hair rise against my lips.

I could stay here all day.
Let time pass on its way.

The top of the mountain is nearing.
With no shame,
I lower my knees before my queen
to cleanse my palate in your spring.

I paint circles around the outline
God took the time to shape.

You are truly a masterpiece.
And she is as beautiful as you are.

This is a sacred intimacy we share.

I rise to meet your lips
and kiss you with gentle intensity.

We stare,
passionately and deliberately,
into each other's eyes.

I want to see your climax rise.
You take what's yours and bring it home.
You explode into rays of euphoria,
and you are not alone.

You are a work of art.
Timeless.
Priceless.
To be protected at all cost.

5.

The Dance of Fire and Ice

Do you hear that?
The crackling sound of fire and ice?
The two do not mix unless you dare to think twice.

There is a mesmerizing balance
in the way they dance together,
like a cozy sweater in warm weather.

Fire brings a warmth the ice has never known,
craving the feeling of love and ease.

The fire,
in turn,
yearns for rest from constant intensity.

They both wonder if this will last.
Eventually,
one must give first.
Which of them will leave their past?

Will the ice be happier as water,
even if it risks losing its shield?
Will the fire become a calmer flame
without losing its passion?
The will to wield.

From something fierce
to something subtle, yet still radiating.

Is it worth the risk to change?
To be?
To see where this new form leads?

The sweet thought of freedom rings,
moving away from something stagnant and cold
into the unknown.

Adapting.
Ever flowing.

A flame,
calmer but still glowing.
Still intense, yet evolving.

But what of the comfort ice has always known?
And the intensity fire uses to grow?

"Take the risk," cries the fire with blazing conviction.
"Take the risk," whispers the ice,
craving moments unfrozen in time.

The ice willingly drips itself
into the fire's hands.

And because of this,
they changed forever.
It was never an ending,
but a beginning.

A brand-new endeavor—
to become what they have always been,
and to change in ways
that will live on forever.

6.

Soldier of Love

In the shadowed heart of strife's domain,
where chaos reigns and passions wane,
my lover's valor, fiercely displayed,
unyielding in the face of danger's claim.

Upon the field, fierce and bold,
his courage rang like legends told.
But now he lies in iron bound,
with thunder raging above ground.

And I,
his love,
ride without delay.
With a heart ablaze; I charge the fray.

Left. Right. Left. Right.

I march to free the one I hold dear,
unshaken by doubt, untouched by fear.

Beneath the moon's cold silver glow,
through broken winds and fallen snow,
I ride where only the fearless go,
to bring my love back home once more.

His image burns like the northern star,
pulling me through from near and far.
With every hoofbeat, I proclaim:
Our love is fierce; our love remains.

Through peril's road, I press toward dawn,
my will a drum that drives me on.
Each stride ignites resolve anew
to break his chains
and carry him through.

For him, I fight.

For him, I stay.
Through every storm, we find our way.

Our wounds will heal.
Our hearts will rise.
Love does not bow.
Love never dies.

Through fire, fear, and endless night,
I carry love beyond the fight.

My heart, my truth,
in the name of true love.
We will always rise above.

7.

Love Menu

Tonight, we will meet at a new place.
It's my favorite kind of night,
we role-play.

We meet where candles melt into wine
and jazz rains down from the ceiling.
As I sip my Chardonnay,
A single finger traces the spine of my back.

I haven't seen your face yet,
but I know those hands anywhere.

Tonight, we meet again as strangers.
I introduce myself.
You take my hand in yours and kiss my palm.
Your touch feels divine.

You take the seat across from me.
We enjoy our meal,
getting to know each other again like it's the first time.
Uncontrollable laughter fills the air.

The waiter asks about dessert.
I look at you.
Hold your stare.
Your eyebrow lifts.
That smile curves.
You already know.

I slip a napkin from beneath my plate,
write temptation in ink,
fold it once,
then twice,
and slide it into your coat pocket.

"No," I say softly.

"I'm saving my appetite."

I rise from the table knowing
you're not far behind.

The ride home hums with tension.
City lights blink a steady green the whole way,
like they're in on it,
guiding us with intention.

When we arrive,
you open my door.
Your hand finds my thigh and squeezes tight.
Then you lead me inside.
When the door closes behind us,
the world stays outside.

Shoes by the wall.
Keys on the counter.
Our coats falling,
my note still hidden in your pocket.

Suddenly, it's just us.
Our bodies filled with hunger.
Heat.
Anticipation.

What's on the menu tonight?
a little of me?
a little of you?
Don't leave me waiting

I yearn to be sipped like wine,
Twirled slowly through time.
I've had visions of my body wrapped in you
like temple-spun silk.

My tongue tracing hieroglyphs on your skin,
signing my name on the dotted line.
I need to be yours.

The depth in your eyes
screams through our silence,

pulling me closer.

Cologne on your collarbone,
humming with heat.

Set the table.
I'll be your dessert.

You know I can't take it when you tease me.
So, I'll give you something
to make you say you need me.

Those rough, working hands
firm and soft around my throat,
working me.
My heart is ready to stop.

Wait.
I want to tell you.
Wait.
I'm trying to tell you.

My mouth opens,
but the words won't fall out.

"He had me.
Had me he.
Tongue tied."

Jill Scott on the speaker tonight.

It's okay.
You don't have to hear me to feel me.
She speaks for herself.
Just listen

She says,
"Control me, for I am yours,
willing to bless you with all you've been yearning for."

I'm serving you a very special menu tonight
so, feast as you like.

Michelin five-star worthy,
I need my entrée.
I've only had a taste.
You, my love,
have yet to clean your plate.

Open the curtains.
Dim the lights.
No—
turn them off.
I want to see the sweat drip from your body
onto mine in moonlight.

It is finally time
to make love like it's the first time.
I leave no crumbs.
I know your toes goin' numb.
Don't give in yet.

The best is on the way.
And I've been waiting all day
to feel my body sway
to the rhythm of you.

I envy your skin,
molded by the formation of God's design.
And it's all mine.

8.
Masked

We made love,
but we did not make truth.

We shared space,
but not intention.

Your body was close,
but your soul stayed hidden.

I convinced myself I could feel you,
even when you were not there.

We moved like strangers,
playing lovers in dreams.

You kissed me like a secret,
with lies dressed in softness.

Love is not always dressed in red.
Sometimes it wears black.
The kind you wrap around yourself to feel safe.
The kind you bleed into
when no one is watching.

You touched me like I was the only one,
but loved me like I was one of many.

And I chose silence.
Because silence was softer on my heart
than holding the truth.

9.

Parts of You

I carry the parts of you
that even you do not recognize.
The ones you pretend do not exist.
The ones you curse when no one is listening.

I held the boy in you who never felt seen,
and the man who never learned how to cry.

I was there in the dark hallways
where you thought no one was.

I memorized your wounds like scripture,
just to know where not to touch.
But I touched them anyway.
And you bled.

I wish I could call it an accident.
But that is what I was here for.

I reached into your shadow
to pull out your light.

It hurts at first,
but soon you will understand
why you need to fight.

I became a mirror
you were not ready to face.
And when you looked in my eyes,
the version of yourself you clung to escaped.

10.

Green Eyes

Your eyes were always brown.
Not hazel, not black,
just warm, uncomplicated brown.

The kind of brown that feels like truth.
Like a door left open.
Like soft ground after the rain.

And for the longest time,
I loved them just like that.

But today,
when I asked where you've been,
something in the way you looked at me
shaded them almost green.

Not in color,
but in feeling.

That deep,
silken kind of green
that coils around your throat like a vine.

I saw something in them,
maybe her,
maybe the version of you
I'm afraid to find.

You smiled and said
you were out with the guys,
but your gaze was empty

Not angry,
not cruel,
just elsewhere.

And suddenly,

every quiet moment we shared
echoed too loudly.

From then on,
I started reading your silences
like warning signs.

Your stillness became a strategy.
Your patience felt practiced.

And I hated myself for doubting you.
I hated how green my eyes had become;
how bitter I tasted
while still calling it love.

But I couldn't stop seeing
what wasn't there
and feeling
what hadn't been said.

Is it really all in my head?

11.

Here Lies

Ring.

Ring.

Ring.

You have reached the voicemail box of—

Where are you?
I've been calling you.
Call me back.

Click.

Day and night.
Twelve of twenty-four hours,
yet somehow the night lingers longer,
and the silence grows louder.

When you are not here,
my intuition feels stronger.
My suspicions have grown larger.

It is almost like I can feel her hands
running across my skin.
The sweet scent of cinnamon.

The sweet, stinging lies
you whisper in her ear.
I can hear them clearly.
Are you really this insincere?

Ring.
Ring.
Ring.

You have reached the voicemail box of—

My intuition is screaming.

Baby,
I know you have a secret.
But the depth of my love for you
will not let me believe it.

And if it is true—
when I have been here through every season,
and I know I have been pleasing,
then there must be a reason
you would stoop so low.

Should I call your mama?
Does she know?

My mind commits treason,
making excuses,
reaching for any reason
why you are with her right now
and not me.

Are you more than just a man?
You were—
to me.

Now I am swimming
in this poisonous river of sonder.
How could this be?
Do you love her?
I wonder.

This desire I have for you
could surely take me under.

I know you have another lover.
From your lips you would never say,
but just like I know the night
could never truly be longer than the day,

I know you would take the truth
to your grave.

But to your love,
I am a slave.

Careful.
Behave.
Come home.
Stop the lies.
Or next comes—
here lies.

Please, do not test.
Where art thou, Romeo?
For I am your Juliet,
and I am not done with you yet.

If you go,
we all go.
We will need eighteen bearers
to take us all home.

Kisses, the phone.
Click.

12.

The Collector

(Epic Poem)

I met the most mysterious man by the river one day.
He was so beautiful,
but in an odd way,
nothing on him was out of place.

I had seen him there many times before.
It was almost as if he studied me,
but he never said a word.

One day,
I went down to the river as I often do,
and for some reason that day,
he slowly approached me.

As he drew closer,
my heart began to beat almost out of my chest
onto the riverfront.
Baboom. Baboom. Baboom.

He laid his hand on my heart,
and I felt calm wash over me.
He asked me my name,
and we talked on and on.
It was as if time slowed for us alone.

It had only been less than four hours,
but somehow it felt like the hours became days,
days became weeks,
weeks became months,
and before I knew it years.

I clung to every word that fell from his lips.
It was like he knew exactly what to say,

and what I was thinking
before I ever said it.

Surely that means he is the one, right?

I mean the natural romance this man possesses
was as if Aphrodite gave him one-on-one lessons.
I was caught in his trance.

I was ready to take the art I had guarded for so long
and give it to him without a second thought.

We learned so much about each other in such a short time.
As the sun began to touch the tree line,
I knew I should leave.

As I stood,
it was almost as if he was afflicted,
maybe even offended
by my ability to withdraw from his magnetic gaze.

He said,
*"Surely, with only a few moments of sunset to spare,
Please stay to watch the stars begin to appear."*

His words hooked me.
I could not pull away.
So, I stayed.

But as the moments passed,
I swore I heard—
Run.

As we lay beneath the stars,
I could have sworn it was the voice of a woman.
I looked around.
It was only us.
I dismissed it.

But instantly,
as if to drown the sound I had heard,
he inched closer and whispered in my ear.

"Tell me," he said,
"What does your heart desire,
so I can shower you with all the love you've ever wanted?"

As he whispered,
I could feel a warmth like fire.
Being the hopeless romantic I am,
I mistook it for the warmth of true love.

I told him,
"More than anything,
I yearn to be loved in a hundred different ways
by someone who takes the time to learn me
not just today, but every day."

—Be careful what you say.

He never gave me his name.
Now that I recall it,
I told him everything in my heart.
Little did I know I was giving the enemy a map
from the very start.

Still oblivious,
I asked him,
"What do you desire?"

He said,
"I have seen all the world,
and I have riches to last the rest of my days.
The only thing I am missing
is the heart of a beautiful woman to steal away."

When I play it back in my mind,
I realize he slithered double-sided truth.
He meant what he said.
I just did not hear it that way.
He did not come to give me the love I was missing.

Had his beautifully articulated mirage of words
not clouded my vision,
I might have seen him stitching.
I might have heard the hissing.

"What is that falling from the sky?"
I asked, turning to meet his eyes.

He said,
"Do not worry about the sky."

And with his hand extended,
he offered me his heart.
It looked almost perfect beside mine.

Who would not accept such an offer of love?
A thing like this only comes once in a lifetime.

But the longer I stared,
I noticed something.
It was oddly larger,
as if he had enough love for more than a few.

And something was wrong.
It almost looked as if it was not beating.
It did not give me that love feeling.

Moments later
I heard it again,
faint at first.

The voices.
Run.
Run.
Run.

He noticed my hesitation.
With impatient agitation, he said,
"I told you I would shower you with all the love you desire.
Give me your heart, and we will build our empire.
I will hold it and never let it go.
Just show me you love me so."

He spoke of everything he would give.
And I listened.

What he said was true.

I gave him my heart.

And then—

Boom.
Boom.
Boom.

The love he promised finally arrived.
What fell from the sky
was not the love meant to keep me on this high.

The mirage dissipated.
What I thought would be a shower of love
was a strategic sabotage.
Love bombs.

He holds my heart in his arms.
Now I see it.
It was always intentional.
He took my heart and never let it go.

He lied—
but he does not think so.

He would say,
*"When you give someone something,
it no longer belongs to you.
You did this to you."*

A closer look at the heart before you,
and maybe you would have seen
the hundreds of names etched into its walls—
a meticulously stitched heart.

He chuckled.
"My art."

The fumes mixed with the fire that fell from his lips,
lit the canteen of his double-sided truth.

That was the final ***boom***.

I should never have given my heart to you.
You think you are teaching me a lesson in love
so you do not feel guilty when you run.

But I did not give it to you.
I gave it to who I thought was you.

You did not want me because I was special to you.
You wanted what made me special for you.

The heart he offered me was never his.
It was collected pieces
from his inventory of countless women.

I spoke.
He listened.
He stitched and chose from his jars of hearts
specifically for me and my wishful thinking.

It may have been his art,
but it damn sure was not his heart.

He was not a lover.
He was a listener.
He was a swindler.

In his home, you would find
a wall of stolen hearts—
beautiful women fallen to his siege.
A memorial that bleeds.

But never had he heard a sound more beautiful
than the heart that beat in me.
He had to have it.
Now his most prized possession.

He moves on to collect the best parts of women
and teach them lessons.

Do not give your heart hastily.
He does not come to give love—
he comes to take it.

Do not be blind.

I had enough love for both of us.
You could have left me a piece,
and I would have survived.

But in his greed,
he left me with nothing—
only the rubble of his love bombing.

Now I am here,
longing to feel the love I once had for myself.
The love I should have never given to anyone else.

Unsatisfied by the love of a woman,
soon he will come again.

Heed the fire of the serpent's tongue.
Guard your heart, or it will be lost forever.

Beware of—

The Collector

13.

Eclipse

Hello,
Moon.

Lovely to see you again,
my sonder sister.

From the darkness,
I heard you whisper.

I came to meet you before next rising.
I cherish the moments we share
before the sun kisses the horizon.

Standing in your moonlight,
the feelings of yesterday
begin to wash back over me.

I never seem to escape them,
just as your gray never escapes you.

Though your light is burdened
by the darkness that surrounds you,
you always remain true.

You hold me in your gravity.

Come,
dance with me.

Oh, the many phases of you,
sister moon.

I see a lot of myself in you.

No matter the face you show today,
you are as whole as the sun.

Just as beautiful,
but somehow there's more to you
than meets the eye.

It's something alluring
in the way you shine.
Your grays illuminate me too.

In this hour,
your shades of gray
fill my room with hues of blue.

When I came to meet you this morning,
I see you chose to show your whole face.
Out of them all,
I love you this way.

A mirror that reflects
the beauty of my own many phases.

Oh, how I envy the stars.
Maybe I shouldn't say.
But see,
then I would never be too far away.

Endlessly shine the rest of my life
in a galaxy unburdened by day and night.

Finally,
I'd get to share with the world my own light.

I could watch you
and sister sun
dance existence away.

With you both,
I share time and space.

In moments she will arrive,
and through my window,
your hues of blue will intertwine
with hues of orange and yellow.

It's beautiful,
the way you share the place.

In this hour,
I too wear my true face.

The mural you paint on my walls
seeps into my mellow heart.

And my,
how that beauty is unmeasured
when we all shine together.

Goodbye, moon.
Hello, sun.

Part II:

Inheriting Fire

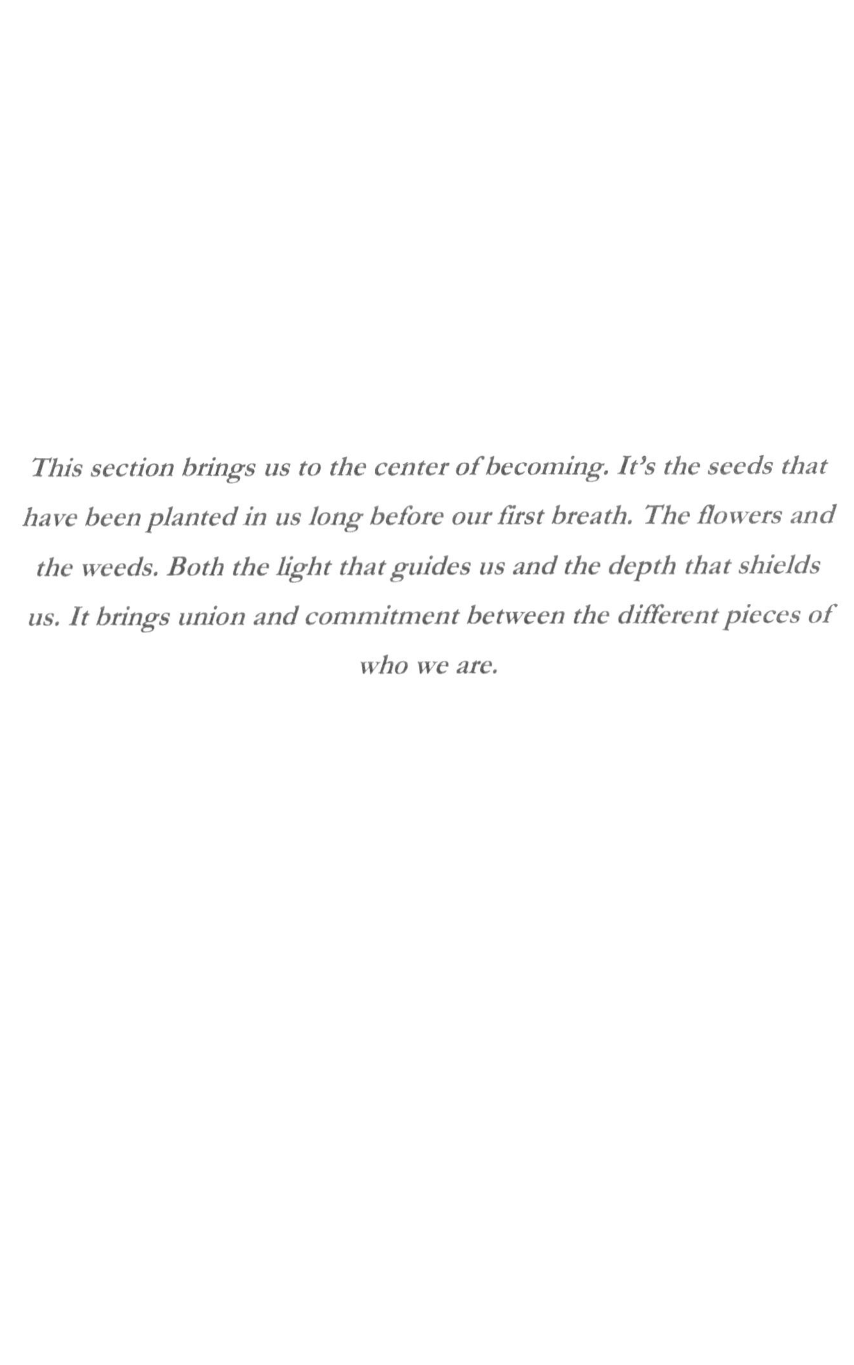

This section brings us to the center of becoming. It's the seeds that have been planted in us long before our first breath. The flowers and the weeds. Both the light that guides us and the depth that shields us. It brings union and commitment between the different pieces of who we are.

1.

The Heart of a Woman

Man,
before you were soldier,
before you were king,
before you were builder of towers
and maker of wars,
you were a son.

Cradled not in steel and smoke,
but in the warm arms of a woman.

The first sound you ever heard
was the heartbeat
of one who bled to bring you forth.

You were fed by her body,
taught by her patience,
sheltered beneath the canopy of her prayers.

And yet,
how easily you forget.

You build empires on her broken back,
carve kingdoms from the marrow of her silence.

Steal her voice and call it order,
steal her labor and call it duty,
steal her body and call it conquest.

Do you not see?

When you desecrate the woman,
you desecrate the very earth that cradles you.

When you silence her,
you silence the echo of your own beginning.

When you strike her,
you strike the garden you were meant to tend.

You lay waste to the only paradise
that could have saved you.

The rot you see in the world,
the bitterness in your chest,
the wars that rage without and within,
they began the moment you chose
dominion over communion,
chains over covenant.

She was not made from the dust beneath your heel,
but from the rib beside your heart
to stand with you,
to teach you again what mercy looks like.

You are meant to mirror her sacredness.

If you crush her,
you are already crushed.
If you enslave her,
you are already enslaved.
If you scorn her,
you scorn yourself.

The wound you carve into her
becomes the famine
that starves your own soul.

Man,
you were not born to be a tyrant.

You were born to be a steward,
a partner,
a guardian,
a singer of songs in the cool of the day

Not a breaker of bones
in the heat of conquest

Kneel—

in the ashes of what your pride has burned.

Look into her eyes—
the mother,
the sister,
the stranger.
See not a thing to conquer,
but a universe you were meant to protect.

Heal her,
and you heal the garden.

Honor her,
and you honor the breath
that first stirred the dust into your bones.

Bless her,
and you will find blessing
rooted again in your own blood.

Because without her,
you are a hollow drum,
searching for the beat.

A lost wanderer
in a barren field.

Remember her.
Return to her.
Rise with her.

With her,
the garden may yet bloom again

2.
Journey of the Dove

Little dove,
why are you crying when you should be flying?

So worried about the outside world,
pieces of you are dying.

Lying to yourself,
doubting yourself,
dimming your own light
so as not to offend others,
afraid to ruffle a few feathers.

Flying through stormy weather,
your tears blend with the rain.
Masking your feelings
so no one sees your pain.

You give people all of you,
leaving nothing for yourself.
Left feeling the only one to blame is you,
but it is on them too.

They do not see you.
Not the way I do.

Spread your wings and fly, little dove.
Do not cry.

Heavy is the crown,
and still, you wear it well.

Little dove,
you have known hell,
but you made it through.
Who are they to tell you about you?

They could not fathom
that someone with so much love to give

has survived through what you have lived.

You tell no one.
So, they know not the damage
that has been sinking in.

You feel everything deeply,
and inside it is hard to manage.

But you pack your feelings away so neatly
that no one knows
what you are really thinking.

You encase yourself
so as not to erase yourself.
You've built a nest inside your chest.

But now it is time
to wrap love around your wings
and give yourself the grace you so freely give.

You deserve all good things.
You have so much more life to live.
More ground to cover.
More lovers yet to discover.

This is not the end, little dove.

You need love too,
you do not need someone else to give it to you.

Your spirit is under attack,
and enough is never enough.
They keep coming for more.

So, take off toward the horizon and never look back.
Show them how high you can soar.

3.

Phoenix

In a world of whispers,
she speaks in flames.
Her passion often runs untamed.

No one in this world is black or white,
more like shades of gray.

People rarely cherish
what they do not understand.

Like how a woman's prayers
can outweigh the trials we stand.

People hold layers,
shedding,
giving,
becoming each day.

Some days she stumbles,
and that's okay.

Many set out to burn her name
to protect the visions of man.

Through fire she walked,
through ash she ran,
barefoot on prophecy.

Each time she rose,
her shadow became
a dragon that soared
through clouds of ember.

As spirit and shadow merged,
a phoenix stirred within her.

When she returned,

her face was unchanged,
but her energy transformed.

She was always herself.
It was your vision that was worn.

She alchemizes each time
and arises brand new.
Still herself—
just reborn.

4.

Abundance

The water I use to nurture my garden
flows in abundance.
Still,
I must fetch it with my own hands.

The light I need to nurture my garden
shines in abundance.
Still,
I must endure the dark nights.

The fruits of my labor
rain down in abundance.
Still,
I must gather them myself.

Worker bees come in abundance,
but so do the creatures of the night.
Still,
I must give it to nature as it gives to me.
I must not fight.

My garden grows only with duality
and how I pour into me.

I had to weed it out.
I had to plant the seeds
that would sprout new trees.

At first,
my soil was rocky,
and fresh leaves could not stand
against the breeze

So, I got down on my knees
and prayed and prayed
life into an empty fountain.

Nothing instantly grew for me.

The water did not just appear.
First,
it came from blood,
sweat and tears.

Then I walked for many years until,
I found a body of water that was clear.
I drank from the body of Creation,
As I did,
I felt roots begin to sprout in me.

When roots grow from within,
they bend whichever way the wind blows.

I am as solid as the trees.
My branches
hold endless fruits and leaves.

My garden will always be beneath my feet.
And as I walk,
I leave my footprints in time.

The world is my garden.
As I walk, I grow.
All this is the will of the Divine,
etched onto my bones.

5.

You Are Seen

You are the kind of beauty
that makes angels pause.

Not for perfection,
but because your heart
still believes in mercy after being shown injustice.

You still weep for others,
even while healing your own fractures.
From a mustard seed,
you've grown entire pastures.

Child of sorrow.
Child of stubborn light.
Child of becoming.

God has seen every silent tear,
gathered each one like a pearl in the palm.

And says:
"I am making something marvelous of you,
not despite your pain,
but because of it.

Stay close to Me, brave one.
The world may still misread your soul,
but the One who made you never will.

The earth called you beloved
before anyone else called you anything at all.

You were never meant
to look like where you came from.

You were always meant
to resemble where you were going.

And oh, beloved,
it is beautiful.

— Sincerely Yours, Shadow.

6.

Memento Mori

If I tell you I want flowers,
will you think I'm less of a man?

Are the only flowers I deserve
the ones for mourning,
wilted on cold marble?

If my forehead receives
gentle kisses in the morning light,
would you see me as less of a man,
or would that be all right?

If I cry,
will you hold my hand,
or do my tears make me less of a man?

If I told you
I yearn to be held and caressed,
would you be less than impressed?

The pressure to always appear
so masculine is killing me.

Memento mori.
True.

But I've decided
I will rewrite my story
and what it means to be a man.

From toxic masculinity I ran,
to discover a new man,
assured in the balance
of his masculinity and femininity.

I deserve a soft love.

I deserve intimacy.
I am still a strong man
no matter where I stand.

The soft rain comes
with powerful thunder.
I don't have to be one or the other.

7.

Those Who Endure

(Voice of Mother Earth)

My precious one,
come sit beside me.

I see your small hands
carrying burdens too large
for them to hold.

You listened for danger,
the way some children
listened for lullabies.
Safe in their homes.

You stood in rooms
heavy with anger.

You watched love shatter
against walls and believed
that silence meant invisibility.

You chose not to shrink yourself,
but instead to go sword swinging.

The weight of that sorrow
reflected in your eyes,
even with all the love you held deep inside.

You believed that being surrounded
by brokenness meant you were broken too.

But listen.

You were never broken.
You were forged.

Not by cruelty.
Not by accident.
But with love too deep
for shallow waters.

Your beauty was never
the beauty of easy laughter
or gentle hands.

It is the beauty of the tide
that returns to the shore,
no matter how many times
it's been pulled away.

This is your land,
your place.

Your face was shaped and spun
by a force unseen,
but eternal.

The light from the moon and sun
was your guide,
but the earth is maternal.

You burn with the quiet glow of endurance.

You carry tenderness,
even after the world
begged you to harden.

Though the mirror lied,
though the world labeled you
"too much"
or "too strange,"

the truth is:
you are rare and you are going somewhere.

8.

Your First Mother

There are some who are born into light.
Their hands are soft.
Their voices are sweetened by ease.

But not you.

You were born with salt in your veins,
the pulls of the seas in your ribs,
the strength of your roots
already carved into your spine.

The world did not come gentle to you.
It came with noise,
with fists,
with cold doors slamming in your face.

It came with hunger and hurt,
with a love that wounded instead of healed.

And yet,
there you were.

Small fists
clutching something ancient.

A little flame,
flickering stubbornly in the center of all the ruins.

I will live,
it whispered.
I will love,
I will make beauty out of this brokenness.
It dared.

The sorrow tried
to tear your roots from the earth.

Loneliness wrapped around your small,

fierce heart like weeds.

Even when your mouth
was too bruised to ask for kindness,
even when the coldness around you
tried to turn your soul to stone,
you refused.

You chose again,
and again,
to lift your face
to the cold,
silver light of the moon
and rise.

Not like a delicate flower.
Not like a golden child.
But like a tide
that cannot be denied.

The child you were,
the little warrior carrying love
like a hidden ember
through the wreckage—
she is still here.

She is watching you
with wide, proud eyes.

She is whispering:
"You did not betray me."

You became what they said
was impossible.

You became the woman
still at war within her own heart,
because she refuses to stop loving,
even when it hurts to stay open.

You became the woman
who feels everything deeply
and yet stays

in the fight,
in the love,
in the living.

You are not ruined.
You are the cathedral
built from broken stones.

Your face—yes,
your face carries it all.

Resilience.
The ache.
The tenderness
not crushed but sharpened.
The quiet fire still burning behind your eyes.

People may not know how to name it.
Some will mistake it for sadness.
Some will confuse it
with coldness and secrets.

But those with old souls,
those who have walked
their own deserts—
they will recognize you.

They will know this truth:
Here is a woman
made not by comfort,
but by the relentless decision to love anyway.

And the earth,
your first and fiercest mother,
smiles every time
you choose to keep burning.

Every time you dare
to be soft,
your tides pull the moon closest to you.

You were not born to be pretty.
You were born to be unforgettable.

You were born to be a song
too ancient for ordinary ears.

You were born to carry
both sorrow and wonder
in your hands,
and shape from them a life.

9.

Andromeda

(Epic Poem)

After a long day
of the intentional distraction of society,
I come to the same tavern every night.

From outside,
I hear belting laughter.
The sound of contentment
from those who aren't about what comes after.

I sit at the same corner table, observing from afar,
capturing the joy and unity of my people
in a way only my pen and paper can.
Sketching the faces of drunken men and a dying land.

It fills me with a bittersweet ache few would understand.

It is only here that I feel free to contemplate my existence
while I draw the faces of those who can bear witness to mine.

But I cannot escape the thought:
if I am always the sketcher and never the sketched,
who will remember me when my time to move on is next?

Surely flesh is not all that I am,
nor all I will become.

As wine, music, and stories of ancient times
fill their bellies,
I continue sketching faces
destined to be forgotten a hundred years from now.

A few short moments later without warning,
butterflies began to fill my own.

I felt her presence before I saw her.
The distinct aroma of her aura
blessed the room before she arrived.

When her grace finally entered,
I was intimidated and intrigued simultaneously.

I turned a fresh page urgently,
knowing I had to capture what my eyes beheld.
Now or never.

But my lines betrayed me.
I erased again *and again,*
frustrated by my own artistic limitations.
My once-confident hand failed me,
unable to capture her light.

Like the sky, her essence shifted.
She was not meant to be contained only witnessed.

I wanted to ask her to stay still,
to freeze for just a moment
so I could satisfy the ache of my creative hunger.

But even in stillness,
she changed.

How does one do that?
I wondered.

Subtle.
Unpredictable.
Divine.

I knew I had to meet her,
to know her story,
to know her origin,
to know her becoming.

But the words escaped me.

Who is this woman, appearing out of the night?
Her shadow danced with her light on the walls.

Her movements braided with music.

A thought bloomed in my chest:
Is this a woman,
or the embodiment of something far more ancient?

She reminds me of Andromeda.

Then I heard a voice,
familiar, but not my own.

"Are you ready now to come and meet me?"

Her words echoed inside me,
yet nothing reached my ears.
She spoke the language of soul,
one until now I didn't know I could speak.

I rose from my stool.
I set my pencil down.

She met me where I was and stood behind me.

And when I turned to come face to face
with what had consumed my pages all night—

Her curls swirled with stardust.
Galaxies danced around her face.
Her skin shimmered with iridescence.

How many colors can one woman hold?

Her eyes were envied by oceans and forests ever green,
a truer brown than the sediment beneath the earth's oldest feet.

I looked around for someone to share this experience with.
The room around us remained oblivious.

How could they not see this woman,
unfrozen by age and time?
It was as if she had transcended form
and become consciousness itself.

It was as if she had transcended form
and become consciousness itself.

Her soul did not live inside her body.
It moved with it,
beside it,
separate,
whole.

"Why are they not amazed by you?
Who are you?" I asked.

"They see only the surface," she said softly.
*"They do not look beyond the skin of man.
I am the soul-force within all of you.
Who are you?"*

Her voice whispered through my body.

"I am just a woman," I replied.

She paused.

*"Is that all you are,
or all you have chosen to be?"*

She reached for me.

When our fingers touched lightning traveled my spine.

Then I traveled through the deepest darkness I have ever known,
until only my thoughts and naked soul remained.

At first,
I wanted to wrap my arms around myself,
cover what had been laid bare.

In the next moment,
recognition washed over me.
All I have inside of me to give and create,
an acceptance that in the end it is not mine to keep.

It is for the soul family to take.

It returns to the fountain that flows within us all.

My quiet thoughts and songs
whisper back into the breath
that comes and leaves each passing moment.

With the walls of my atoms peeled back,
my frequencies sang in unison.

All the people I swore I never knew
yet, somehow my soul remembers.
Light and shadow rose together.

Her voice echoed in my mind:

*"You are to be.
You are to feel.
You are to learn.
You are to change.
You are to love.
You are to live.
Then you are to give back
all you've been given and have taken."*

My body dissolved into a knowing
that I now *innerstand.*

Only by separation can we become whole.
Together, we are.
Together, I am.

You are never forgotten,
a river forever flowing.

She is the breath of the Creator,

the force of consciousness that keeps us going,
the Vita,
the Zoe.

As for you and I,
we are one in the same.

I am Atom.
I am Eve.
I am breath.
I am sound.
I am soul.
I am someone.
I am no one at all.

You cannot be lost
if you were always found.

I come from a collective source of energy—
my people,
my plants,
my animals,
my galaxies,
and generations before me.

I am within all of you.
You are within me.

How can I be just a woman
when I am everything?

When I opened my eyes,
night had fled the tavern.
With the rise of the morning sun
came a new life and a mind no longer afraid to remember.

10.

The Remembrance

I cleared the table
of the dinner we never got to finish.

I rest the plates in the kitchen sink.

I look up to see you outside,
pacing back and forth to blow off steam.
Standing at the edge of yourself.

There's an instinct inside of us all
to save and protect the ones we love.

But how do you protect
someone from themselves?

I know this battle all too well.
Family,
Friends
or lover,
I cannot be your savior.
But my arms can be a cover.

How can I fight a shadow
only your eyes can see?

War within oneself
is one hell of a thing.

I cannot see your chains,
only the smile you painted on this morning.

You wear that mask so often
you've begun to forget your real face.

But I remember.

I want to pick up your shadow
and lay it beside mine in the meadow,

and share with it our light.

To share with the deepest parts of you
what it means to climb,
to align,
to be whole
with the parts that had to learn the hardest lessons.

Do not resent your shadow.
It held up your defenses.

If you ask mine,
she'd say,
*"I did what I had to do
so your light could survive in you."*

The first step to peace
is learning that shame and guilt are not the same.

Only one brings awareness.
The other is pain.

Shame divides,
but it does not conquer.
It holds you hostage,
binding you to a yesterday that no longer exists.

Waging war against the parts of you
most desperate for love that doesn't dismiss.

Behind the veil of your shadow,
a flame burns fierce enough
to consume you from the inside out.

Trust me.
If you allow it,
it always does.

I know that fire.
I've heard whispers, too.

Most days they didn't whisper.
They screamed.

They demanded to be heard.

Maybe now it is time
to ask the right questions—
like how loudly you would call out
to someone running in the opposite direction.

11.

Countryside

(Epic Poem)

I'm a country girl.
What can I say?
No shoes outside on a cool summer day.

In fields of dandelions and lavender,
my brother and I would play.
Dancing here, there, everywhere.

While Mama blew bubbles
into the sweet spring air,
wish flowers landing gently in her beautiful brown hair.

And at night,
the lightning bugs would come to play.
We'd roast s'mores and sing the night away,
music humming from the radio as we fell asleep.
You beside me caressing my hair in the dark.

Sigh.
The country air.
I'd wake up to sneak strawberries out of the fridge
Flood you with a million questions about the world.

So curious.
I wanted to know all the wonders.
I miss you, Mama.
I miss hearing you sing.

With you I felt free,
like a baby bird on new wings.

The country reminds me of you.
So does the color blue.
Your eyes, deep and true.

But the ocean—
the ocean is truly you.

Fierce.
Limitless.
So many hues of blue
for every shade of you.
So many layers.

Take me back to the country air,
before the war.
Before the fear,
the screams in the night,
the bruises and cries,
the goodbyes,
and empty promises of better times,
the ones that never came.

No one is to blame.

You know what they say,
love and war.
Damn.

Here I go,
making excuses again.

I can't save you
from your sin.

I was given the gift to create a life,
but I cannot save it.
But in my heart, I knew
I shouldn't desert her.

So, I followed you,
sword swinging

Win or lose,
I shared your scars
because I stood with you.

A mini you,
clinging to your leg
like a pocket blade.

Should you lose this battle,
I fall with you.
Warrior of flesh,
but my spirit survived.
Thank God I'm not dead inside.

Now
I rewind the reel in my mind,
trying to find the missing pages.
How much of my youth has been taken?

So much to say,
the things no one wants to hear.
This pain,
my dear,
has been a lot to bear.

Wise beyond my years.
There's a reason.
But every soldier has their season.

And my love for you has always been clear.

Mama,
let's go back to the country and stay there.

We didn't have much,
but we had each other.

You taught me a love that knows no bounds.

Even at the expense of me,
you'd burn cities to the ground.

I'm grown up now.

I hope you understand.

Soft by nature,

but hardened by the hand.

Nightmares of war.

Rise, child soldier
who's been ready to lay down her sword,
but clutches it still in fear.

Heart in one hand,
sword in the other.

I can love like no other,
but at the first sign of danger,
one comes after the other.

That's how I survived.

In love with those I've loved.
Blind leading the blind,
but that wasn't your crime.

Generations of broken women.
Single mothers doing the best they could.

And now,
I am a mother.

And it is time
I should turn chains into ropes,
climb up out of old ways.

Changing the hues
from shallow blues

to baby blues.

Breaking rules
in the name of generational wealth.

The next generation I bring
will have stronger wings.

Today,

I unwrap the old wounds that still sting.

The memories I suppressed
so, I wouldn't disturb your illusion.
To avoid bleeding on the ones
who mean the most to me in honest confusion.

I'm cleaning out and stitching up
the parts of you and I that I can no longer carry.
The spiritual baggage
that was never mine to bear and bury.

I lay it down.
The bags that were once so heavy,
I've built the strength to hold steadily.

I'm ready
to release these burdens.
I hope you're no longer hurting.

12.
Seeds That Sprout New Trees

(Dedicated to my son Nezaryi)

I made from scratch
a heart that radiates a love so pure.
Beautiful skin and growing bones.

I made you from scratch.

Your fingers and toes.
Those deep eyes, full of wonder.
A spirit that started as a seed rooted in me.

You are made of my own flesh and blood.

Just a thought,
as I put you to bed caressing your soft curls.
I am forever indebted.

I made you from scratch,
but it was you
who breathed life into me.

With your first breath,
I became alive.

I'm awakened after all these years,
and you still teach me.

It is I that owes you.
Something.
Everything.
And you owe nothing at all.

One day my vessel will leave you
for some time.
But I walk with you forever in spirit.

When tomorrow doesn't come for me,

remember these words:

We are eternal.
Energy only transforms.
Two parts of a whole.

My vessel will set
with the hues of the sun.
My spirit will rise
with the hues of Mercury.

The nexus was cut at birth,
but the bond between mother and child
remains a puissance
no blade can sever.

I meant it when I said this love would be forever.

Our spirits intertwined,
Aries and Gemini.

The ephemeral days
I wish would last forever
will set with the sun.

When your vessel sets
with the hues of the sun,
when your spirit rises
with the hues of Mars,
we will find each other again.

I will take care of you
until then.
My love.
Take care.

I made you from scratch.

13.

Both Sides of the Moon

You see her smile,
but never the cries
that echo through her soul at night.

You admire her strength,
but never what it costs.

She is an anomaly,
a riddle written in the stars,
a paradox wrapped in breath and bone.
A wanderer but never lost.

I see her
the way the earth sees the moon,
one side glowing silver in full view.

The other hidden,
holding its own secrets,
yet still willing to reveal them.
Two truths can live in the same body.

She is as soft as the hush of dawn
and sharp as a blade.

She is the calm in the eye of a storm,
and the storm itself,
rising wild against the shore.

She belongs nowhere,
and everywhere at once,
a bridge between contradictions,
a woman yearning for more.

She can be both the light
that warms a wanderer's face,
and the shadow
that teaches them to search for depths.

The world may try to name her,
to choose one side,
but she cannot be seen from one angle.

Or even understood
in a simple language.

She is both wound and healing,
both question and answer,
both sanctuary and wildfire.

And like the moon,
she will keep turning,
revealing only what she chooses.

Her power is not in being understood,
but in being infinite.

14.

Depth

Humans,
why are you afraid of humanity?
When does depth become humility?

It's as if the fear of depth breeds insanity,
as though depth itself were a calamity.

Death is not meant to be a one-way street
when you leave your ego at your feet.

It is the transition
from without to within.
To die
is to live again.

The powerful seek immortality.
True power is knowing
you are already immortal,
because you are only a kindred spirit,
a part of a soul's purpose.

Running.
Running.
Running from an end
that only brings you back to the beginning.

So, if you spend your life
running from what you're feeling,
is your soul really winning?

Isn't that the end goal?
Nobody really knows.

I like to think
that when I go,
my possessions become lessons,

my bones will sprout new trees,
but my soul—
only my soul comes with me.

This vessel is a vehicle
carrying me to my next destination.
This body holds a nation
lived in by my ancestors before me.

These freckles,
this brown skin,
this melanin,
passed down through generations.

When you look at me,
you don't see one woman.
You see a nation.
You see its basic anatomy
that I carry all that in me.

The chains of society,
like a leash around my neck,
suffocating.

But the key
has always been inside me.

So, I breathe
and let it all wash over me.

I am not afraid to swim in deep waters,
even if that means carrying the world's opinions
on my shoulders.

So why are you afraid of me?

Because I am brave enough.
Because I am courageous enough.
To swim through the sea,
letting waves take me and wash over me.

Tough enough to be tossed through rough waters
and still rise—

again *and again.*

I can weather storms
because the fiercest storm lives within.

And if I can master my emotions,
nothing can master me.

My mind,
my heart,
my spirit
all belong to me.

This skin I'm in
belongs to the Earth.
It does not belong to me.

So, hear me when I say
until my lungs no longer breathe,
I wear my heart like a badge of honor on my sleeve.

She doesn't follow me.
I let her lead.

The thought of knowing I can escape illusion
and find sanity on the other side of these waves,
gives me the strength to swim for days.

At first the salt stings,
but it keeps you afloat.
Salt clears my vision.
Strengthening my soul is the mission.

Beyond the storm
lies still water.
There,
me and all my emotions set sail.
On the other side,

I meet another side of myself.

Come with me,
I can carry us there.

Him, her, me and you.
I can get us through.

My purpose is to bring you closer to you.

Surface was never enough for me.
Surface dwellers are my greatest enemy.
I belong to the water.

All respect for these troubled waters.
I have a wondrous spirit.

I want to explore your heart.
Show you how to turn pain into art.
Show you how to release control
and let the waves roll.

I want to explore the deepest parts of you.
Let down your guard.
Let me near it.
I can show you how to really feel it.

Because where I'm from,
we begin and end as spirit.

I walk the world inside out,
my skin pulled back to show what lives within.
The yang and the yin.
Blood.
Flaws.
Faults.
Experience.
Heart.
All in the open.

Hoping you'll meet me at the water's edge
so I can give you the courage to go farther.

Come.

I've walked in your shoes.
Our feet share the same bruise.

Better to swim,
because those who run always lose.
chasing their tail,
gripping tightly what they're fated to lose.

You see the scars from every demon I fought.
Mind and heart
battling for my soul against the pain I've known.
Better to fight the devil you know.

Made in the image,
and God stands with me.
When I go deep,
I know who waits there.

I walked through hell
to rise a phoenix.
Mask where?
I don't need it.

I am not afraid to bleed in the open.
My ego needs no stroking.
My pride is unprovoking.

I am a soldier
for all those around me.

I pull people from the chains of mortality.
I raise morality.

In life,
there will always be duality.
But it is up to you to have faith in humanity.

Do not let your spirit be calamity.

We are beings of feeling.
Our bodies are only sensors.

We feel pain.
We feel pleasure.
We feel joy.
We feel rage.

We feel cold.
We feel warmth.
We feel love.
We feel low.
We feel high.
We feel until we die.

For this,
there is no magic potion.

So, feel your emotions.

PART III:
The Call Is From Inside

This section reminds us how thin the line is between the past and the future. Our will to choose what it truly means to be human. It challenges you to explore what your life means to you. Highlighting the ways we limit our self through comfort and convenience. Through lines in the sand that don't naturally exist. I am challenging you to choose the print you leave on this world today. Will you consume or create?

1.

The Beaten Path

(Voice of Creation)

I know it is lonely sometimes.

I know the road you walk feels narrow,
steep, and stony.

I see how they have turned their faces from you,
how even those you called
brother, sister, or blood have doubted you,
mocked you.

Misunderstood the fire
I placed inside of you.

I told you it would be this way.
I told you the world would not always recognize my children
and curse them for the roles they will play.

I told you the sword would divide the closest hearts
on even the sunniest days.

And still, you said yes to Me.

You stayed when it would have been easier to run.
You stayed when it cost you love,
comfort,
belonging.

You stayed.
Beloved, listen.

You are not lost.
You are not forgotten.

You are exactly where I have called you to be.

The path I carved for you
was never meant to be easy.
It was meant to be holy.

I do not build my warriors out of ease.
I build them from fire,
water,
and relentless mercy.

I build them with the weight
of long nights and unanswered prayers.
I build them up when the world breaks them down
and they choose to rise anyway,
with Me as their only light.

I know you are tired.
I know you wonder sometimes if you are truly seen.
I know the battle inside your chest is heavy.

But hear Me.
I am not far from you.
I am not ashamed of you.
I am not disappointed in you.

Not one moment of your suffering is wasted.
I have braided your pain into purpose.
I have sung over you in the dark hours,
when you thought no one heard.

I have written your name where no hand can erase it.
The world will not always understand,
the strength I am forging in you.

Let them turn away if they must.
Let them call you strange,
too much,
too tender,
too fierce.

You are needed here.

I see the hidden wars you fight.
I see the prayers you offer
with cracked lips and a shaking heart.

I see, and I am pleased.
You are not walking toward defeat.
You are walking into the fullness
of who I created you to become.

Stay close to Me.
When the night grows heavy,
lean into My chest.
When your hands tremble,
let Me steady you.
When your voice falters,
let Me sing through you.

You are not an orphan.
You are Mine.

And no betrayal,
no sorrow,
no silence
can steal you from My hand.
Those who turned away will one day see
what I was building in you all along.

But for now,
take heart beloved.
Walk on.
You are not walking alone.
I am with you until the end of the age—
and beyond.

2.

Children of the Divine

(Epic Poem)

(Voice of The Children)

The air tastes like iron.
Every breath is a weight,
a reminder that lungs were not made to breathe dust.

I sit in the rubble,
small knees pulled to my chest,
on the broken edge of what used to be my home,
the floor cracked open like an old book
my father will not read anymore.

Under my bare feet,
a small piece of happiness remains,
a remnant of the flowers my mother planted.

I bend down to pick it up.
For a fleeting moment,
my pain disguises itself as peace.

Oh, how beautiful they once were.

As I stand for the first time in a while,
the numbness leaving my legs,
something flutters across my feet.
A torn page from my brother's schoolbook.

I fall to my knees again,
reminded of my reality.

My sister's doll hand
reaches out of the rubble
like a question no one will answer.

Above me,

the sky has forgotten how to be blue.
It hangs low,
heavy,
swollen with smoke and sorrow so old
it hums through the bones of the earth.

When the sky breaks
loud,
hot,
and angry,
I run into the smallest places I can find,
like mice hiding from hawks.

I used to know the names of every flower that grew
between the cracks in our street.
Mama taught me.
She said,
"Even the smallest things bloom when they are loved."

That's why I feel safe
in this tight, quiet place.

Until I look back out
and the flowers are gone,
and the street is broken.

Down the road,
a woman calls for her son,
the name caught in her throat,
half hope,
half wound.

Last night the ground shook so hard
it felt like God was weeping beneath us.

Today the sun sets
not with gold,
but with a bruised kind of red,
the kind that stains your memory.

I do not know where my brother is.
I do not know where the sun sleeps anymore.

I wonder if the children in Hiroshima screamed
when the sky tore itself apart.

Are those of us who did nothing to blame?

I smell smoke in my hair.
I taste metal when I breathe.
I'm sure there is radiation in my veins.

I saw the fear in my mother's eyes before she left,
a mirror I could not turn away from.
I don't think she's coming home.

I used to dream of becoming a teacher,
or someone who plants gardens.
I still dream sometimes,
though the dreams feel thin now,
like paper.

I only have crumbs in my pockets
and a string from a kite
I haven't flown in a long while.

Mama still sings in my head when I'm afraid.
When there is no more bread, she sings.
When the windows break, she sings.
When my friends' names are whispered into dust,
she sings.

Her voice is soft, even now.
She says,
"Hold on.
Hold on.
God sees you."

In the silence between explosions,
I can hear it.
A kind of prayer stitched into the dust.
Not words exactly.

Just a wanting.
A reaching.

I close my eyes.
The ground hums beneath me,
a sound so low and deep
it feels like God's heart breaking.

Somewhere far away,
men in clean clothes sign papers,
talk of borders and revenge,
as if wars are chess games
played with children's bones.

Somewhere far away,
the rich pour their wine,
laugh into the night,
safe behind their gates.

Here,
we drink from our cracked hands.

Here,
we learn the different silences:
the one before a bomb,
the one after the last scream,
the one that fills the empty chair at the table.

I wonder if they know,
those men in suits,
how fast dust climbs walls,
how sorrow seeps under doors,
how easily gold tarnishes when touched by blood.

I wonder if they hear us,
all of us,
across years,
across broken cities,
across languages,
whispering the same aching song:

Before the towers fall.

Before the oceans rise.
Before even the stones forget your names,
don't let this happen again.

I sit here breathing dust,
feeling the weight of a thousand lost voices.
I press my hand to the earth,
and it shudders under my palm.

Even if the world forgets,
DNA reaches below the soil,
deeper than any man could dig.

In Gaza,
a girl presses her ear to the floor,
listening for the footsteps of her brother
who left with a stone in his hand
and never came back.

I wonder, Gaza,
are your walls dust now,
is your bed the earth,
do you stare at fireworks that never end?

In Ukraine,
a boy sits beneath a crumbled bridge,
counting the cracks in the concrete,
wondering if it was worth it.
The flags,
the shouting,
the men in polished suits
who promised glory that came with graves.

I wonder if the mothers in Ukraine
howled into the smoke,
searching for the names
they whispered into cradles.

In the Congo,
a girl wraps her arms around her little sister,
hiding her from gunfire.
She dreams not of castles or riches,

but of a morning where no one runs.

I wonder when the Congo wept,

exploited and young,
and brothers lifted guns instead of each other,
if the rivers carried the tears of their sorrow
all the same.

In Yemen,
parents gather crumbs from the street,
whispering prayers into dust,
not for victory,
but for bread.

I wonder if in Yemen
the children hiding under broken beds
counted the footsteps of death
and wondered if the ground would ever stop bleeding.

In Sudan,
children weave stories from smoke and memory,
building houses from hope
because stone and wood are long gone.

I wonder if the children in Sudan
count the drums of gunfire at dawn,
mistaking war for thunder
and still pray for rain.

In America,
they told fathers to fight for honor,
told mothers to be proud of coffins draped in cloth.
They fed us songs of loyalty,
stories of enemies we had never seen.

In the slums of forgotten places,
in the ashes of fallen cities,
in fields where blood fed the soil,
we, the children, call out with broken mouths:

We were never meant for this.

While we bled into the ground,
they built higher walls.
While we wept in the night,
they counted coins by candlelight.

We were never meant to know
the smell of burning bodies,
the taste of hunger's silence,
the sound of a door kicked in at dawn.

We were never meant to draw maps with guns
or write history in the language of wounds.

They taught us to worship borders,
to forget that the earth has no lines.
They taught us to kneel to leaders
instead of lifting each other.

We know now:
the enemy was never the human across the border,
never the one who prayed in a different tongue,
never the skin,
the land,
the song.

The enemy was always the lie,
the whisper that said we are not the same,
the hand that reached for power
and crushed the lamb beneath it.

And yet here we are,
carrying the bones of dreams
through streets that forgot laughter.

We do not want your medals.
We do not want your flags.
We do not want your wars.

We want the gardens you paved over.
We want rivers you poisoned clean again.
We want the sky before it burned.

We want to sit together.
The child from Gaza,
the child from Ukraine,
the child from Congo,
the child from America
From every scarred corner of the earth

and sing one song,
the first song,
the one the earth hummed
before anyone drew a sword.

I am still here.
I am still dreaming.
I am still hoping,
even if my voice is small,
even if my feet are tired,
even if the flowers never come back.

I will not forget how to love.
I will not forget how to pray.
I will not forget that once
the world was meant to be beautiful.

And maybe, someday,
it will be again.

And still—
we hope you will listen.

3.

Creators House

(Epic Poem)

(Voice of Creation)

The house I built for you,
I shaped with My own hands
and called it good.

I poured rivers through your bones so you would never thirst.
I planted gardens where the wind could rest.
I scattered stars so you would remember
you were never alone.

I gave you the land as a gift,
not a prize to be seized,
not a beast to be broken.
I told you to tend it,
to keep it up,
to love it
as you would love your own breath.

I taught you the Sabbath so the soil could breathe.
I taught you Jubilee so the poor could rise again.
I taught you to leave the edges of your fields for the hungry.

I taught you to lay down your swords and lift one another instead.
I never asked for thrones.
I never asked for towers.
I never asked for crowns made of gold and altars of fear.

I asked for gardens of fruit and flowers.
I asked for mercy.
I asked for hands that build instead of burn.

But you did not listen.

You built empires
on the backs of the poor and called it a blessing.
You carved kingdoms
from the marrow of the land and called it progress.
You lifted your fists and called them holy.
You sharpened your swords
and marched into the fields of My children,
crying My name over their graves.

You turned My house
into a marketplace.
You turned My sanctuary
into a battlefield.
You turned My words
into weapons and cut your brothers
as Cain cut Abel,
then knelt at altars built on their blood.

The rivers choke on your waste.
The forests are torn open like graves.
The air shudders beneath your machines.
The ice weeps into the sea.
The deserts crawl forward like blind beasts.
The sparrows fall.
The whales sink in silence, drinking poisoned water.

I watch the free will I gave you rise in hatred.
Still, I grieve it.
Still, I gather every tear your Mother Earth cries.

The earth remembers Eden.
She remembers when you walked barefoot without shame.
She remembers when your prayers rose like mist in the morning.
She remembers when you spoke to rivers as friends.
She remembers when the mountains bowed to shelter you.
She remembers when love was law.

Now she carries your wars in her soil and on her walls.
She swallows your dead.
She bears your sorrow in her sea.

She groans beneath the weight of your forgetting.

And yet she still prays for you.

Every storm
is a cry of mercy.
Every quake
is a mother calling her children home.
Every fire
is a warning written in flames.

You traded the breath of the earth for silver.
You sold the living water for profit.
You poured out the cup I gave you and filled it with blood.

I offered you the bread of life.
You broke it and sold the crumbs.
You crowned yourselves with iron and fire.
You hoarded grain in high towers,
while My little ones withered in the dust.

You built walls of fear and locked the door
on the stranger whose face was My own.
You passed by the wounded on the road,
humming songs about salvation.

You made kings
where I asked for shepherds.
You made wolves
where I asked for donkeys.
You made markets
where I asked for mercy.

Still, I stand at the door
and knock.
Still, I wait
for you to unlock.

Return to Me.
Let the fields rest.
Let the rivers run clean.
Let the forests sing again.
Let your hands remember how to bless.

I am not in your towers.
I am not on your thrones.
I am not in your wars.
I walk among the broken.
I weep with the wounded.
I kneel beside the poor.
I breathe in the dust of your ruins.

In the darkness,
I am your light.

My covenant remains.
My words remain.
My love remains.

I carved your names into My hands.
I have waited centuries for your return.

Choose now whom you will serve—
the hunger of your own hands
or the heart that first breathed life into you.

I am enough.
I have always been enough.

4.

Judas

Judas was a man,
tired,
angry,
afraid,
wanting things to happen faster,
wanting a kingdom he could touch,
wanting certainty more than surrender.

He followed with hands that trembled,
with a heart wrestling with its own darkness.

He loved,
but not enough to trust.
He believed,
but not enough to wait.

Thirty coins felt like justice,
like control,
like making something happen
when heaven seemed too slow.

He did not know
they would taste like ash in his mouth.

And even now,
Judas still walks among us.

We trade the breath of the earth for fleeting wealth.
We betray our brothers and sisters
with policies,
with purchases,
with silence.

We step over the poor on our way to bigger gates.
We strip the land bare.
We poison the water.
We lift our fists,

where we were meant to lift our prayers.

We kill
and call it progress.
We hoard
and call it blessing.

Who still kneels among
the least of these,
bleeding quietly in places we refuse to look?

And like Judas,
we do not think we are betraying,
not really.
We are just trying to survive.
Just trying to win.
Just trying to hold onto what little
we believe we deserve in the end.

But silver always burns.
Silver always slips through trembling hands.

And when night falls
and the garden is still,
when the olive trees no longer extend their branches,
we will wish
we had never waited.
We will wish
we had trusted.
We will wish
we had loved more than we feared.

But there is no buying back a soul
with the coins it was sold for.
There is no unbreaking the heart we traded for comfort.

Only the mourning remains.
The hollow echo of a kiss that tried to bind the Infinite.

5.

Walk With Me

(Epic Poem)

First, we lay down our swords,
not in defeat,
but in defiance of endless hunger for blood.

We tear down the flags
that taught us to fear our brothers.
We step over the lines drawn in dust
that taught us to fear each other.

We scatter the coins
they used to weigh our worth,
measure our love and buy our silence.

We walk away from the noise,
from the hollow towers,
the marketplaces of lies,
those drunk on power.

We return to the soil,
barefoot,
calloused,
forgiven.

We plant gardens in the ruins.
We sow seeds where empires crumbled.
Tomatoes where missiles once fell.
Wildflowers in the cracks of the concrete.
Grain in forgotten fields.

We gather not by nation,
but by need.
Not by color,
but by compassion.
Not by profit,
but by the law of giving.

We gather not by nation,
but by need.
Not by color,
but by compassion.
Not by profit,
but by the law of giving.

We remember the Sabbath,
not in stiff buildings,
but in the hush of the forest,
the swell of rivers,
the resting of our own weary hands.

We stop unnecessary machines.
Let the fields breathe.
Let the animals heal.
Let the tired earth
sigh into her seasons once again.

We trade not gold,
but in bread, labor, and songs.

We rebuild with our own hands:
small homes,
open tables,
fires for warmth,
not for war.

We teach our children the true stories:
how every living thing bears the fingerprint of God,
how no life is owned,
how every neighbor is kin.

We make no dictators.
We forge no crowns for kings.
We bow only to the quiet voice
that speaks in wind,
in heart,
in the dream.
The voice that once walked with us
in the cool of the garden breeze.

We become wild again,
and holy,
and wholly free.

And when the old world screams at our backs,
we do not turn.
We do not fear.
We do not kneel.

We know who we are.

The ones who found
the milk and honey
hidden in the spoils of what once was.

We are the branches,
the seeds,
the living temples.

We are the Kingdom to come.

And when you do finally arrive,
the first thing you notice
is the quiet—
not the heavy silence of mourning,
but the living hush of a world finally at peace.

The rivers sing again.
The trees lean closer to the sunlight,
branches stretching like arms waking from a long sleep.

You walk barefoot through streets
with no walls and no borders,
only gardens woven through the stones,
children laughing in every language,
their voices blending like rivers meeting at the sea.

No flags fly over these fields anymore.
Only prayer cloths,
bright and fluttering,
tied to ancient olive trees.
Gifts of color not conquest.

In the markets,
no coins are exchanged,
only stories,
labor,
fruits,
smiles.

A woman from the mountains
gives bread to a boy from across the old sea,
not because she must,
but because his hunger is her own.

The Sabbath is not a single day now.
It has settled into every heartbeat.

The land rests
because our hands have finally learned to trust.

There is enough.
Enough wheat.
Enough water.
Enough love.

Because we no longer hoard.
Because we no longer fear.

You pass a garden
where old enemies kneel together,
planting seeds.

No one remembers whose blood
once stained this soil.
Only the harvest is shared.

The ocean breathes slower now,
healed from the poisons we poured into her veins.

The birds have returned,
their songs stitch the sky with gold thread.

No one locks their doors.
No one builds towers
to make themselves higher.

The highest place
is the low table,
where all are seated and fed as one.

And at the center of the city,
where a thousand churches and temples once fought
for the tallest steeple,
there is only a single wide circle of stones,
open to the sky.

There is no roof between us and Heaven anymore.
There is no war here.

Only the steady,
breath-filled chorus
of a world that remembers.

We were made for wonder,
not for walls.

We are not strangers anymore.

About The Author

I, KaLaura O'Ram was born in the month of June 1999 in the heart of North Carolina, the only daughter among five children. A self-described black sheep of the world, but never in the company of a pen and a page. I began writing at the age of nine, first crafting short stories in the hidden corners of life.

I have always been deeply sensitive to the world — to its beauty, its ache, and its quiet cries. I experience life in layers and have spent my life translating that feeling into something sacred and spoken. Though I have lived through my share of abuse and trauma, I refuse to be defined by survival alone.

I am who I have chosen to become through it.
I have often felt like I did not belong to places, to people, or to the role others tried to assign me, based on my experiences in life.
Regardless, I have always maintained a sure sense of self. I have always belonged to language, creation, and to the invisible thread between the soul and sky.

My inner world has always translated best through art. I am deeply passionate about God, about the power of creativity, and about the journey and destiny of this planet and every soul upon it.

I believe humanity is divine kin, bound not only by blood, but by breath.
I bare my heart and spirit openly and unapologetically on my sleeve.
I write for those who do not yet have the words.

Every life carries a story, and this is mine. I offer it in the hope that it will help others feel, remember, and embrace their own.
I stand for love. I stand for peace. I stand for unity.
This book is a collection of poems written across eighteen years of a life still unfolding.
I offer them to you now, whole.

Contact and business partnerships:

Email: mypoetscommunity@gmail.com

www.ingramcontent.com/pod-product-compliance
Lightning Source LLC
Chambersburg PA
CBHW031301130726
47988CB00007B/2671